A Life Song Between Two Worlds

By
Francis Boni

T0015105

The City University of New York,
1997

Front Cover:
The Song of Love, 1914,
by
George De Chirico

CONTENTS

Introduction

As we know, poetry itself is a mode of communication. Thus, in the themes of this episodic, poetic work, I attempt to wreak, with the imagery of an imagist, yet still Neoromantic in spirit, my thoughts and feelings upon metaphorical expressions; specifically, in their pregnant construction, with reflective, emotional rhythm, they attempt to deal with some crucial meanings of life, its baffling paradoxes hard to resolve or to accept, and above all, with its destructive problem, still without a real tentative or effective solution, of violence in our present century. These interrelated ideas or themes form a unity of poetic strain and, for this reason, this poetry is poetry of ideas, purpose—poetry with a message; a dynamic blend of ideas from which one grows out of the previous ones, almost like a ripple effect, expressed in a dialectical relationship in an intensely passionate way, and their philosophically burning issues in dramatically and relatively abstract, symbolic terms. It is therefore at this point that the title, *A Life Song Between Two Worlds*, reveals the author's state of the soul, not as a retired closet philosopher, in dealing with those paradoxes and dilemmas of life, which assume that A and non-A do not exclude each other as predicates of the human situation, but by painting from nature and starting with the individual being or event or real before him and its present history, although, at times, with great allusions to the ancient heritage shedding light on, enlivening and informing the present. Only by understanding or standing close to and by being influenced by the despairs of the human situation, embedded in the present living reality is the moment for the author to make his conscious transcendent leap in order to blend imaginatively the metaphorical meaning with the physical or literal. In other words, he represents the world which surrounds him by means of the world that is in him, and, perhaps, above him, too. It is the duality of these two worlds which people attempt to reconcile at different levels-unrelated images, phenomena, events taken out of their everyday context and set in a peculiarly organized whole which reveals tentatively their inner reality and again, perhaps, their ideas of the supernatural aspect of reality. Thus, every event, object has two aspects, the normal one as one perceives it; the other, the spectral, the metaphysical, without pretensions for the author, which can be realized only in the transcendence of the human endeavor. Furthermore, on a personal note, the author, being born in the Roman Campagna of Italy, speaks more than two languages fluently, and thus he is actually, at times, between two worlds of thought, yet resolved into one by thinking multiculturally. Finally his concept of dynamic love, indeed, ultimately turns toward the divine, but it is, above all, a love in action for humankind. It is a prayer in principle which turns into a courageous love in action trying to touch someone else's silent love. Therefore, all the author wishes and hopes for these existential poems or spontaneous outpourings of sensibility is that they generate a spontaneous combustion of love in the reader's soul.

Francis Boni

A Hero's Life

There are no great men
But only great challenges
That "authentic" spirits must meet
To overcome
Not only personal fears
But also the dreads
Of that unknown and unconscious reality
Which manifests those challenges
Through which they become villains or heroes.

Epigram I

When a stone falls
On a person's head
He certainly knows
How deep is the pain;
But when an idea falls
Into his head
He never knows
How deep is its pain;
Paradoxically, if an empire's walls
Always start from within to fall,
Then it is rather droll
When a unity in diversity seeking
That a man should be looking at from without
What he should be looking into from within,
For the hard from the latter always comes.

And what is dead cannot be experienced

But is expiated with

The unheard–of, grievous experiences of one's fate,

But yet one is no more alive

Then when one is facing those facing death.

Dedicated to Prof. Ernest Nagel

Working Like a Devil

(The Renewal of the Promethean Oath)

I lucubrate alone day and night
Without giving a claim
To Lucifer to bear me light

Since to bring about his fatal fame
Rebelled against the divine love-command,
So unwanted is his proud flame.

The pristine dignity of man I commend
In between the twilight of matter from model
Creating life as an unbound craftsman,

Knowing himself as an honest devil under no spell,
Disinterring truth and destiny into one's hands
And rising above the waste land of Babe'l.

Therefore, fellow men! be it your delight to scan:
God bestowed Promethean love upon common sense
And all else followed by the light of its own ken;

This also was the essence in His son's reverence
For all, equally warmed and lit by his humane reason
Of being of a fire-soul benevolent to their essence,

For, if they love it as one person,

That person is God and man,

And that's the soul of my Master's arcane lesson.

It

(The Mystery Of Love)

If one can't define "it"
Why should its unseen powers be illustrated?
We all believed in it without seeing its pit
Since the arcane world was for it created.

What naked and prestine Eve forbiddenly bit,
But embraced and clad herself with,
Reductionists ravished with the fallacy of their wit
As they also did with goodness' pith,
Since SATAN rebelled against its divine writ
And the LAMB made gory atonement for it.

Where the wild Adriatic washes,
Not Aphrodite's magic with fresh lashes,
But the dormant skulls of old
And yields Rimini's shore radiant of gold,
The sweet stroke of the love-intoxicated Francesca,
Crying out, not in sheep's clothing, vendetta,
Restored its status quo *di novo moto*
With the storm and stress of the romantic motto:

Why, why that which is the source of so much joy
Becomes the cause of so much great sorrow?
Knowing no way out of this existential decoy
Except "learning to love" being the art to follow.

This is the activity which destroys all anxiety,
For separateness is the ruin of all humanity
Keeping love from bearing its genuine unity
And then its ultimate oneness with divinity
And so love is the consummating circular economy
In a real and splendid harmony.

The Poem of Fire-Love

If in the midst of true splendor I am

Shading off the absurd pain

In anguish of the living

About the abyss of despair drifting,

Not lucifugous as a bat I am,

But luciferous and igniferous,

Since, in the profound, of Prometheus I am

The flaming neo-romantic archangel, Gabriel,

Not chained to the fruit of the land

Like a fallen angel, but kindled

By a spark of divinely rhapsodic frenzy

Harbinger of the good news

That LOVE, infused in us, must,

In every aim, time and place,

Always be with a raging FIRE rekindled

In the very recondite, resurgent roots of the heart

Under the poietic vow to be solitary and solidary,

As that hanging by a hair of a quickening artist

By nature tearless and fiery,

That the luster of their burning blaze,

Sprouting from the heart's somber and tangled wood

To light novel Life and Art

Bound to reveal the journey of the epic, eclectic smile

Of its passionate will for justice on earth,

Will glow like red coal-eyes

Flashing radiant stares of marvels

To crush of pain

The perpetual and Gorgon nightmare

Of which the experience of its nameless sufferings

From the humane spirits alienates and rives

The human spirit, like the despotic and foul crimes

Against mankind of our violent times

Which the dignity of that spirit ravage and deprive

Of the humanization and democracy of Love

With the beast in man that is Satan,

Its ardent snake lying in the grass always

Ready to snuff out the Promethean conquest

Of its living light of faith.

The Ladies Ws at Elaine's

As their plastic comings and goings
Noisily strut the floor at Elaine's,
The Ladies Ws are formidably vain
Who deem not to be pushed
But to push the laws of man.

Yet their shrewdly sane businessman
As vamps molds them with a puppet's mien
Tantalized to reach the sap of his secret domain.

Now will they ever reap the fruit of his promised fame,
For no one-eyed king leads the blind bat to the end,
But only Elaine sees the foul aim of his game.

Those lured on with the prospect of Moses' land
Could not the struggle for success forsake
As the grass must even grow above the hot sand.

Those struck by the bondage violating the body's sake
Tried, instead, to apostatize the racket of a rake
For the quest to redeem their debauched make.

But alas! too late for their remake,
The business must go on, don't forget!
Regardless what scarlet claim is at stake.

Just as those gallant nights recurred with cakes
Cut at Elaine's tables in various shapes,
Likewise Ladies Ws were cut in similar respects,
For their misconception of the *Law of Effects*
Indeed was their original mistake.

The Uncertainty Principle

It's very easy to fall into hell or uncertainty,
But not at all easy in heaven or into certainty,
As the falling on the moon of a fair florescence
To carry a spice of life on an orb without fragrance
Where not even brooms blush on its arid muddiness,
Once a source of mystery for its hazy whiteness.

Many people, without faith, shipwreck into vagueness,
For in this vagrant banality they seek sureness,
The complacency to know of a wave only the appearance
And not, as a searching wind, its inner difference
Sweeping it away inshore of safety,
As does to beauty as well Eros' levity,
Yet ever-receding into itself in a sea of obscurity
Leaving philosophers and scientists in the irregularity
Of the laws as far as they refer to its reality;
Nor can they ground the flow of its induction,
For, if they could, it would become deduction.

The flower with the wind yet bears richness,
But not, in the quest for truth, final salvation
To learned ignorance seizing with its finiteness
That uncertainty is certainty's groundless foundation
And not the methodic doubt of "Je pense, donc Je suis,"

As seen with a known mass of pollen with known velocity

Levitating in the wind to bloom again into indeterminacy,

The ever-unfolding harmony of a beauty's interiority

Mocking, with its fresh and redolent sweetness,

Even at human death laughing with cocksureness,

For, of this event, humans have no consciousness

But only the anguish of its uncertain nothingness,

Not quite unlike that of an artist in taking a chance

Upon the critical striving for unity in the balance.

A Trivial Pursuit

In a fleeting moment of my history
Like a drop in the sea was Willoughby*.

There was she, a TPD, at the bottom of its hierarchy,
Fair but fearful to be,
Of necessity to bear but not to flee
Its treacherous duties of Science and Humanities.

Resolved she was to pursue the academic view,
Yet to succumb she had to its mediocrity
Which taught things neither ancient nor new
But stifled only the sacred course of maturity.

All was vain to overcome that stale impasse
Turbid with ignorance and violent happenings
And by the dim vision of authority overcast
For showing a glimpse of those far better things
With the help of reason endowing all of us
And proudly saying: veni, vidi, vici.

* Willoughby: A Junior Public School in New York City.

18

Thinking

There is no irenic solace
To soothe or still this unrelenting soliloquy.

We can find no route to escape
From that unknown penance of it,
That doom at birth bestowed upon us
To deliver mankind allegedly from chaos.

Any living attempt to wipe it out
Is Sisyphus' rock reaching the hilltop
Endeavoring to bring only his absurd fate about
And the haunting presence of its eternal recurrence
Whence springs 'the relentless stream of mind'
With its kindred spirit of endless Time.

With the loss of its sense
The question "To be, or not to be" ends,
Its virtues become clownish nonsense,
Yet its ghostly essence never suspends.

Hence, on the Golgotha is only angst of thought
Until the vainly supreme of human effort
To arrest its river-flow for the sea of the cosmos
Is superseded by Philo's Logos.

To my sincere friend, Ugo.

Ode to an Old Joy

When my flat of one big room and a half
Was with high-spirited minds invested,
They painted its white walls red,
And, at times, the town when they were out,
With logical formulas and idiosyncratic slogans,
While my personal books on the table, soiled with sweat,
Bled for my underlining their lines in red.

Often sunken in a chair, there was Allan,
Forgetful of the ongoing tasteful endeavors
Teasing our minds with roarings of young lions,
Uttering, while the forgetful drug of the food relishing,
With opaque wisdom that our wild pursuits of flow of spirits
Amounted to nothing and not to a flow of mind,
Our discursive and musical bent was nonsense
Or it was feeding the vanity of our ego only,
And his best discourse with dispassion was, of course,
That "there are those who think and speak but do not eat
And this is   sheer nonsense indeed;
But there are those who think and sit
And do not speak, yet they also serve and eat,"
And this is what makes sense for the present
To those eyes which on hedonistic beauty feast.

For the rest of us all, almost appalled,

That appetite was not a sobering Carpe Diem at all,

But it was, for us, a heavy meal with a heavy odor,

Since we indeed at heart believed

That silence, at times, on philosophical matters is truly golden,

Or that the best discourse upon music is silence,

Yet its full enjoyment or communication is measured

When its message is set to practice or to drama,

For love without action is, like idle rumors, hollow,

And so when music from the heart's strings

Is embodied in a jaunty or heroic dance,

Like Pat and Ted in their noble but wild tango dancing,

With a rose alternating in their mouths, in an agony of trance,

This is the silent music of the heart beating within the mind

And bringing a carol to every party of life,

Especially to us with boundless wishes, then, a young crowd,

When youth and health made out of everything happiness

Writing off a neighbor's selfish and frigid calls or speculations

Of the mind in the relentless flow of time

Or the sterile intrusions of frozen stiff institutions,

But freely interacting and choosing with joy

Outwitting our destiny but not fate, and flowing

From one heart to the other and filling the present aura

With sounds of the immortal, and never with the likely, story

That the energy of life can be recreated only without pain

By our inner joy razing the smitten agonies of the brain

And cannot ever be destroyed

From the hallowed ground bass of its real glory.

An Elegy for John

In a sunless and hapless day of autumn life,

From the sober nature of his modest stature

The benign and mature soul of GIOVANNI

Has departed;

Oh what a great misery has befallen us

At Prospect Heights!

For no more

Its laureate teacher of English

The boards of the halls of learning

Softly shall be treading.

Can this apostle's humble splendor

Unlamented go?

Or ever be forgotten

By the colleagues or by the students

For his love for the humanities

Sacrificing, with the last measure of devotion,

His pleasures in pursuit of excellence,

As in being a friend, indeed,

Of all, and, most of all, in time of need?

Truly,

Among the noblest of his friends

No praising tongue can be tamed,

Nor yet among the gods of heaven

In whose lap he now rests

For snatching him too fast

From the breast of his breath

Helpless to breast their fateful waves,

For they dearly loved him

In their mysterious ways

For his humane and indelible deeds

Carving them with his patience and tenderness

To better serve those people's needs

Who will be haunted always sweetly

By the smiling, sincere and fair memory

Of his gentle and silent spirit.

Farewell to a Lady

In the midst of an exhilarating life,
Her beaming comeliness the vanishing point crossed
Which once radiated the fair poise
And the deep-lying emotional joy
Of its daring, exhaustless, vibrant force,
Yet unsuccessful in outwitting the claws
Of a dark destiny
With a victory nothing short of marvelous
Averting the swoop of her captivating grace
From us, as a vulture does with a soul's carcass,
And thus for a car accident
In the city that never sleeps bade us farewell
From the anguish of alienation of this mound of hell.

Farewell, then, sweet lady of gainly shape
Enveloped in a mist of a short-lived past!
Whose transfigured vision in agony
Has suddenly so young reached,
By the car of the sun, the great beyond,
A mystery baffling any quest pursuing its meaning
And bereaving relatives and friends
And even mere acquaintances
Of her kindly and smiling presence of mind
Overcoming with its keen talent social traumas

24

Visiting, in the School System, many students' life.

Farewell, farewell dear shipmate of flowing locks!
Unquiet echo and wake in our lone, sailing hearts,
Like those of lone mothers,
Moaning and mourning your absurd and forced flight
And controlling in their shattered tender fabric
Their petty misery ever breathing
Within their living memory.

A Farewell Epigram to a Friend

True men are rare

As a true love and a true friend;

And yet they come, they see and they conquer,

But they also gently go like comets

Leaving a wake behind

So that we, as real and devoted friends,

Can be reminded that the great or the rare

Was not born but made

By facing those challenges of life

To reach the unreachable heights,

To dream the impossible dreams,

So as to bring amid randomness harmony

And to orchestrate with comity people's tender feelings

With variegated, multicultural melodies

And yet keeping their indigenous pitch of individuality,

For, " if it sounds good," as the jazzy Duke said,

"It is good," even for the chanting soul in thralldom.

Was not this the quest

Of that principal leader

Who launched hundreds of teachers

Against many scholarly obstacles

To become one for all and all for one

In meeting the pressing requests

Of his educational, cardinal nest?

For this craft, no doubt,

He is a formidable maestro of the Art

Who had to express farewell to us

For a far and better humanitarian task,

But never, never with his mighty heart,

For, had we never met him,

Or had he never, from us, parted,

We would have never been so broken-hearted.

To the memory of my dear friend, Gianfranco Bianchi; Summer 1988.

On the Summit of Mount Gemma

While standing alone as an atom fulgid of life

On the bright green and majestic back

Of this rocky, arduous elephant

Capped by a wreath of clouds,

Beneath a cubic cross of steel

Rocking for the strong northwest wind

And touching, with a sad memory, a string,

After a prayer to my late lamented friend

Who soon this nature's breast left

Unripe and panting,

I lower my brow

To gaze downhill

At a vast and vague, gemma-variegated basin

At which center my town lies supinely therein.

From afar looms up before me

The faded red, jagged and flat,

Of the tile roofs, which jagged melodic figures,

Sunken and bounded by the thick, wavy sea-green,

Are as straggly shards displaying life signals;

On the left, narrow serpentine windings

Tracing the road about the Lepini-mountains,

Whereas, on the right,

The Tower and a bald, rounded top

Plus my delectable mount's projecting brow
Upon which the royal eagle made the eyrie once.

Still and lonely appeared the immense background
Whereto almost body and thought got lost
Into its unknown gulf, but the relief
Of a sudden and weak church-bells' ringing
Whose echoing was to the height climing
Set me free,
In front, from that magnetic attraction,
While, in the rear, from the distant
And luring murmuring of Circe's Sea,
That I, for the dubious fright of both sides,
Ran to join the others who stood aside
And off the true affections memorable of the cross.

Ignorance

For us whole human beings, at the beginning,

For whom ignorance cannot be equated with stupidity,

For it's not a state of bliss but of latent darkness

Which one should not gloat over its misery,

It must be asked, in our deep consciousness

As the last refuge of humanity, with insistence:

Have we learned from our past mistakes ever since?

Have we grasped at least the lesson

From our past experiences not forlorn

In the personal unconscious?

Have we understood, for instance,

That relationships require give and take,

Yet that of love is quite different in nature

Since its giving does not require at all receiving?

That it is indeed in the desire of giving

That we are expressing our true self-giving

Or upon the water our bread throwing willingly

And from the deep clamor within the human condition feeling?

When nothing of the kind has us overcome,

Which still our vision darkens,

Nothing has been learned of its outcome,

And in dread one goes on to make,

Of course, the same irresponsible mistakes

And so absurd and incendiary violence

Continues to manifest itself

In the hatred of the racial strife of the human race

Since we haven't yet profited from the sage's message

That he who understands nothing, loves nothing

And can do nothing and so he is worth nothing;

But he who understands something of the inner or outer reality

Also loves, perceives and respects from his lowly station

Breaking, like the blind, the isolation

With many a stranger and friend

By rising together to their relations without frustrations.

Is this the terrible tale which the glimpses of the moon

Of Santayana's History attempts to tell

Or on us impress, yet we, humans as such, refuse to accept?

That ignorance is the heaviest weight on people's head

Which attracts them often to commit

Their greatest senseless bestiality on earth

By pitting brothers against one another

To leave them with wounds which cannot be healed

And the fond heart cannot forget, and yet

The collective unconscious proceeding by changes

Is predisposed to forget

That those who don't look into their life

Or don't learn from the faith of History are doomed

To replay their rhythm or in the snake pit to stay.

To that effect, friends, young and old, to know dare

And make, as soon as possible, many mistakes,

But from them soon learn with a resolute pith
To shake off the glittering ghosts of their distressing weight
From your torpid and haunted head
And to make them no more by turning the tables,
Going beyond their willful repetitions with no creation
For a greater imagination orchestrating with innovation
Where lies the run of the heart and mind
Frantic with joy their faculties exercising
For the chance of one's potentials realizing
And not any longer putting to death
Even the Author of life out of ignorance.

To My Black Madonna

Is she the black madonna of the icons
Painted with a black dress and mantle on the head
Enveloping the gentle and motherly gaze of her face
Transfixed on her son's colorless love for mankind?
Or is she my lady of color standing out for her humanity
For whose heart my heart beats a syncopated rhythm
Of restless and variegated feelings
Seeking the fulgor to win of its grace fleeting
Which very often it blinds me with its purity
And escapes the fulfillment of my burning velleity?

Yet the smile enigmatic of her sweet black and almond eyes
Does not deny that she is attracted
By my vile but sincere desire trying to become
A fulgent fire of love cleansing every acquired shame
Surging from the unconscious' smoldered flames;
Nor does it wish to hide the beauty of the fact in parables
That one should be patient with the dear things of the heart
Which the mind cannot figure out,
For they will, sooner or later, come about
With a hope which always expects the unexpected,
Which is ready to dismiss greed and disrespect
And to let love go and fly free about
The complex and intertwined branches of the tree of life

In search of making a peculiar nest for itself

In this rotten and plastic society of thick violence

Where unequal races should live together

With the irenic blessing of Light immortal,

For, if love were never ours from its inception,

It will never come back,

But if it were ours from the inception,

It will surely be back

To this last democratic hope of the earth.

In Praise of a Roman-American Rhapsody

AVE ALMA ROMA IMMORTALIS!

The roving gladiator saluting thee today

From the world's bloody and violent arena

Is not about to die, but cherishing the illusion

Of moaning the mourning of thy PAX ROMANA,

OH LONE MOTHER! born of thy republic stola,

Noble wake of empires dead and rising!

And controlling his bursting anxiety

In his broken breast for those in agony.

·

He is now an orphan ravenous for thy heart far-off

Who turns to thee in spirit of thy memory

To find comfort in telling the memorable deeds

Of thy honorable people of old

To unequal people who know thee not,

OH ETERNAL LUSTER!

Cast within a cluster of round hills

Filled with a gaiety of restless pealings!

On one the awesome Colosseum with wild circus games,

While on another the serene Vatican in holy festivals,

And all brooded over by balmy pine-trees

To the ancient Appian Way leading

Beneath them an echo of glory wakening

Of the legions' triumphant trumpets and feet

Marching to the Capitol valiantly;

And that thou art his native shore,

Seat of the soul of the sacred wings of the eagle

And for thy common and open pattern mistress once of all.

Goethe's source was thou of a lifelong light,

For Keats and Shelley a ravishing sight,

Forever inspiring, of natural delight,

While for Byron and Browning

A carved name in their souls,

But, for me, of Nature the land

Of genial sunlight which breathed forth,

As the greatest of the past commands,

Laws and Love as concrete universals to conquer all.

The Jus Naturale et Civile of thy will

To subdue the proud and help the needy

Along with the civic virtue of subduing

Self-interest for the country's common weal

Were only with an imaginative leap wielded

By the PAX AMERICANA with agile equity and dignity,

Leading off with Washington, like Cincinnati*,

As father of the country cast in a heroic mold,

Who disposed of his military for the glory marching on

To meet with a plebiscite the needs of a new reality

Of creating a REPUBLIC of, by and for the people

With the eager pursuit for all in a multicultural pot

Of happiness, liberty and equality

Instilled in its progeny's frontier and artistic spirit,

Like that of Lindbergh or Gershwin,

To be a daring aviator or a jazzy composer

Of the people and for the joy of the people

And loved by their novel democratic vistas

Under the wings always of the bald eagle

With a fresh birth of ragtime freedom ringing afar

Off the plantation chants and songs in thralldom.

SIC TRANSIT ROMA!

SIC TRANSIT AMERICA?

Let us pray "ain't necessarily so,"

In these times that men's souls with a complex faith try,

That we, the living, shall not be so greedy

As to drag down America's democracy with us

As the men of Rome did with the zeitgeist of her past,

For, without its feeling of compassion, a kratocracy,

Another monster of cruelty, will await us,

And let us learn from her legacy still

To enlist under the star-spangled banner of freedom

And to commit less tragedies nascent of a mobocracy

Fostering the perishing of the leadership of peace

Of our brave NEW WORLD from the earth

And say: DOMINA! in this twilight wilderness!

MISERICORDIAM TUAM, OSTENDE NOBIS

ET SALUTARE TUUM DA NOBIS.

CINCINNATI*= Cincinnatus, Roman general and statement (519-439 B.C.)

37

Magnificat

There are no poetic or words of praises
To magnify thee, Soul Mother of all mothers,
Of all creatures, thou the worthiest and holiest!
Whose grace and succor are entreated
For quenching the wish
To see our heavenly bliss,
Through the divine light in your translucent eyes
Refulgent on our sorry state,
By imploring thee with a contrite and clean breast
With all the resources of the genius of the language
Failing to unveil the sublime purity
Of your mercy or understanding,
Perhaps grazed it
Only by the paean in Bach's Magnificat
At the moment of filling with good things the hungry
And the oboe with melodic and florid melismas
Dissolving us into a delirium of joy
Beyond all verbal and tonal boundaries
Mystifying every thought and feeling
In contemplating into your highest pulchritude
The presence of the Eternal Verbum,
The finite instinct with infinity,
The mystery which baffles every understanding,
But it turns us, instead, to glorify,

In our inward and humble way,
Your most luminous name,
Of blessed Virgin Mary!
For your devout womb rose
To the loftiness of the occasion
To give rise to
The blossom of love of our profession.

Eternity for a Moment

Pray, oh vague moment about the moral cosmos!
With a baffling and fleeting nature,
Stop and rest for a moment by deserting the enemy
And let us enjoy, you and me,
Our living present as the eternity.

If you glide away with the inflexible pace
Of unceasingly another succeeding,
I will die thousands of ephemeral deaths,
Until the actual one, released from dread,
Will be quite unexpected from your process,
And to endure bravely until the end
The actuality of this brave new world
In every corner ravaged with gory and waxing violence
Of warring beliefs is not a childish game,
For shattered amid the dead lies peace.

Inscrutable your silent direction is,
And yet you are restlessly and evenly flowing
Neither into the womb of time nor of time immemorial
But in a continuum-event everlasting
Which is, at once, dyed
Either by a transient joy or dazzling misery
On faces furrowed with big tears

Settling in the deep of your endless odyssey
About the heavens' cosmic concavity
Where violent events shape the landscape
Of myriad of galaxies.

As you see, stay for a moment aimless wanderer!
Stand still against the wheel of Ixion!
Don't be a part of the flux escaping to infinity
From which is exempt only eternity!
Your immutable, specious point is sweet,
Sweeter than any of your mobile, identical twins
Which are indiscernible in the continuum of existence,
For you are mine at least, like in a black hole,
A still collaborator in relishing statically
My labor of love bathed in the horizon of torment,
Whereas that of deity bathed in a serene silence;
Or a bright loveliness in nature prehending
Loved by the human striving in a distressing silence
By not scrambling with me like a living being
And cutting me off from my love within.
You truly are a friendly and single interval
By my mind, dreamt up eternally durable
Until this isolated creation ex nihilo is shattered
By the anger of the high authority of Nemesis or Plato
With his spaceless dimension of aeonian time,
Or of the fourth dimension of world-events of Einstein
Laying claim to your finite duration and mine

To manifest your unrepeatable life and mine
In the face of the ever-present shade of Time
As a life moment of frigidity and inanity
Fading away, like an irretrievable speck of dust,
In the abyss of its organic infinity
And our short-lived bond splitting
For eternity.

Human Silence

In the heart of a clear night,
Under its wondrous star blaze dancing on my eyes
And lightening its cope above the woven black lies
Of violence of the day and where right and wrong
In the life of every star never lies,
When all about is silent in the living image of change,
Like the slumberous moon now on high
Stark in the dark in peace roaming
With no dog at its snow a bark intoning,
Suddenly the primordial reality of being arises
With the immense and solemn and superhuman silence
Of its seeming, eternal, terrifying shade
Swallowing up the spanless vast of heavens
And the silence of my openness wakes;
The same that ghastly of the frosty grave,
Of haunting Lemures naked, the unconscious dreads;
Whereas that of God's breath is beyond one's depth,
That dismal of some human is within the breadth
Of some feeling eyes, in a wandering silence
Sensible of the buffets' depth of the human state,
Often vicariously faring in a woeful quandary
Because of the muted shriek in an unspeakable terror
Of a bleak heart poignantly bristled
With the fierce echo of a motley horror;

Yet, at times, they are in an attic silence

For not baring the silent joy or smile playing

On the lips of a frail heart coy of erupting.

On this overwhelming transfigured night screen

Some piping voices of agonizing silence lingering

Out in the limbo between my seeing and dreaming

Preyed upon by the nightmare of reason

Might be sailing,

But not one wistfully eerie I feel plying within;

While for a mirthful or wretched heart

Of human sympathy in need

Its silence which is not golden

Must be broken,

It is indeed a golden mean, when makes itself felt,

For the one deep love-worn

Anguish-stricken by its deep, yearning silence

To touch another tender and naked silence

With the stillness of a cat's graze

Turning around the corner of a wall gracefully,

The synapse of an intense feeling

Into the silent, great sea of human consciousness

Or of the still, yet life-giving finger

In the breathing CREATION by Michelangelo.

The Song of a Maiden Nightingale

Just before the midsummer lingering twilight
Eclipsed the vista of the flush of sunset,
The winsome manners and infectious charm
Of your varied and tender vesper song,
On wings of joyful wood-notes
Which all sorts of gloom conjure away,
Oh serene dryad of my dream!
Its melodic invention invited me to sing,
Without the remotest chance of competing,
With my liquid and lucid verses
From remotest depths springing.

Never a lovelorn song mourning, but the fancy perplexing
By ornithological allusions winging,
Perched prominently on a branch smiling
As an inviolable and refreshing Spring
And in shades of a Botticelli's leafage peering,
Her idyllic and pristine call of the afterglow
More inviting and compelling and careless
Than the call of the wild
Had no animal or mortal flee
From its entrancing, canorous trill
But had us all hark and gape at
What flutters and gives us

Joy and despair at first sight
Freezing the pellucid thinking of the mind.

The uncannily elusive melodies of her vocal grace
In the hidden soul of her pastoral symphony
Sweetly warbled their iridescence more clearly
By their sensuous and vibrant notes
With passions softly tinging and counterpointing
Whose beauty I gently drank in from their flow unceasing
So to overwhelm my heart with bated breath
By delightful anticipations and throbbings
That I praised the wisdom of the Almighty
To have such heavenly organ made
A creature not virgin of human desire
That descends unbidden to the ground
By combing precision with grace
In accord with the physics of Newton's apple
And the gainliness of love of attraction
Of which the fruition will come about
Only when my begging is ripe
For His prevenient grace
To let our virtuous and winged desires
Fly together as birds of a feather
In search, with the genial instinct,
Of a dreaming nest with the falling of the dusk
As the owl of Minerva spreads its wings in flight.

Dedicated to my attending Physician: Dr. T. Lansen

Autumn in Valhalla

While the gust shakes down
The diffused and multiform auburn leaves
From the scattered and piled up trees
Leaving them bald and with horripilating branches
Spreading as electric wires over a sick patient
Ready to attract a bolt from the blue
To quicken a sick body to its proper function,
I tread on their solitary lanes,
Strewed with a bloody, yellowish still-life,
To reach Valhalla, the center of Medical Heroes,
To regain, through their intervention, my head's sanity.

Contrary to the tenets of a wont faith
This dead season's movement raises the ghost
Not only of an eternal Requiem
But also of one's loss of health, beauty and brain;
Yet, for nature,
It takes shape of a spirally recurrent cycle,
For green leaves will bloom again and again with nerves
As a thick crown on longevous trees;
Likewise their twig will sprout again when clipped
Until their roots have the sap of organic matter,
But it is understood
That a new tree needs a new seed

Like life for a new human being.

The human, however, is at a disadvantage, ·
For no flowing locks grow back on a bald head
Nor a new leg if someone is amputated
But an afflicted or unhealthy body
Is at the mercy of those Hippocratic knights
Whose dedication and art of Auscultation
Often relieve the piercing crying of patients
From the agonizing pains of their ensouled heart
And diminish at least a little
The overwhelming and profused sufferings
Plaguing pervasively our terrestrial dark orb
With the hope of restoring to the frailty of life
A rosy and live auburn color.

Michael

Opposite my bed there is one sick lad;
I am sick, too, but never as this stranger
That my soul in anguish
I could not feel
Looking at this odd-looking face
Not in any agony for its misery.
There he lies immobile with a sunken back
Lifelessly attached to the mattress,
Like a low relief embossed in a frame,
The wedge-shaped stomach barely pumping still,
As I descry a foreshortening of his muscular frame
With a wide torso upright totally unscratched,
Yet his fixed head completely bandaged
With a spent and impassive face partially dressed,
Striped by tubes plugged into the nose and mouth
Without ever upsetting the dormant, unwinking eyes
Quite unaffected by the sprightly signals or calls
Of the caring and eager nurse
To awake him from a forlorn coma-state.

Every visiting relative, too, tried for long
To call with persistent affection his name,
"Michael! Michael! me boy, oh dear boy!
Answer, please, at least once, me boy!"

Wishing and willing him in a keen to come forth
To the threshold of consciousness or of pain
To give them forlorn hope just for a moment
That his body was still motile,
For his inert bearings yet they refused to accept
Or, as humans, could not accept,
But all wringing tears and begging from one's heart
Were all in vain against the decree of fate,
For the car accident withered this young driver
Fatally of any responsive sensory activity
That I suddenly started pondering
About my better state
In contrast with his, almost lying in state,
And laid a case, before so many of the same,
As his true friend in the struggle for existence,
Before the canvassing conscience of the living:

I knew his name,
I was aware of his absurd and vegetative life,
But he was bereaved of mine,
And perhaps never regaining a taste for its mystery
To let us come across again one day
And together say, beyond all understanding,
Those who lay and suffered together on a stretcher
Also conquered God's fathomless grace.

In Memory of Guelfo Nalli

At the indomitable call of the divine horn

On the golden wings of the chariot of shining Apollo,

Like that of the horns in unison

Which transports the soul, far from every sorrow,

Into a world of mystery and dream

And through which Schubert

At the very opening of his Ninth

His final farewell foreshadows,

You Friend!

Citizen first of Supino and then of Argentina,

Like that great spirit with no silver locks still,

For a painful disease past bearing

Unfurled the wings of your soul to that region.

As the motion of the heartbreaking lyricism

In that symphonic music with fluent ease and no adagio

Is a continuous crescendo and andante,

Like the sorrow of a wanderer, towards twilight,

You, too, son of creative fire

Of the heart mad with pain of your father,

Faithful friend of the departed one of my father,

Continue to stay sadly to the fore

With your mellifluous, canorous sound

In our hearts forlorn and not in the moldering grave,

That had I, like Orpheus,

The holy talent of the enchanting sound

In my heart wherefrom springs,

In its ecstatic uttermost profound, Music and Love

Casting over the brave's grave their transfiguring veil,

Even I would like to try in human shape,

Something hardly ever tried, with a kaddish to charm

In the realm of the celestial spirits

The Supreme Maestro of the universe

So that you might in spirit come back

Once again to play heavenly the holy strains

About your town's windy and rocky valley,

Which we sorrowfully left as innocents,

Wherein the echo sweet and entrancing of your horn

Which confounds the hearing of the incredulous

With a weak flesh and awakes that of the indolent

May bring more Joy about, the inner harmonic rapture

Without which all else is incomplete,

Not to the sacred birthplace only as if the only in mourning,

But also around our spinning-top divided and lightless

Which of it in dire distress is for its race riots,

And thus, with you and Schubert, we, enemies to inhumanity,

Blend together in a unitive vision with prophetic spirit

To mourn the farewell to the quietus of life fleeting

With the quietude serene of the opening theme:

Andante

2 Hns. *p*   *pp*

Death

From the cradle to the grave
When life is not some carved tombstone-dates,
But, in between them, the taut dash of its odyssey
On strenuous, passionate, graceful and tense faces,
This absurd and relentless thought
Of excruciating uncertainty,
This worm in quiet despair in a vicious circle
Within our cage at birth as a live beast,
Not even unconsciously lets us be
With its sneeringly convulsive and bond lot
Keeping us company with psychosomatic traumas
Through the similar lot of an inflicted thought
Like a flux festering in the montage of the psyche
Which always flows towards the ominous reefs,
Falling sheer to the sea, of the first
And lashes them with lifeblood 's plangent breakers
Beleaguering their island
· Of stark stillness of the shades,
For surviving the fixed thorn frozen with dread
Of being swiftly and at bay, sooner or later,
Swept away by the first
Through its silent but ghastly wave,
Like a nobody's written name
On the face of the torrid strand.

Never steeped in sleep but incognito,

At our frailest moments in the dark unconscious,

With an unallayed rage against life,

It hounds and bedevils us, and our grief stiffens

From the breast snatching away with pleasure

All our courage, cheer and faith

That a true mother, in the cradle, has in us embedded;

Oh poisonous, sightless shade my heart fretting

Bit by bit with your dragging march to the scaffold!

You will come and cut off at a blow

Even my eyes for weeping

Not only over my furthest sorrow of the Dies Irae

With the hazy but impending anguish of its fate,

But also over that of the fading beauty of my lady

Withering in the agony of your twilight,

Wispering amorous sighs of lonesomeness

For my arms' glow longing for filling its aching void

And keeping her company before the grin of your void

With scalding tears of affection

Pining away over her gentle soul

With the wrench of being wrested

Soon out of the throbbing pain in her frail breast,

But yet bravely going like an unwavering light

Toward the sphinx of your dreary lot

And your death for a fact,

As already taught by a man of sorrow

To silence it with the silent riddle of love.

Aimless Living

Is so melancholic, verging on despair,
A living that is vile and boring
That its inner anxiety
Is always more vile growing,
For the unknown reality from without
Little does to make a troubled existence smile
To the seeming beauties of nature
Panting to reach them
Like winsome shooting stars;
A stony fate without stars,
Or a blind destiny about a lurid space
Wandering from spring to spring
Wherefrom it can never drink,
Like Tantalus' torments,
Their waters, quenching the thirst for truth,
Avidly sought by its tireless and woeful thought
To pierce through their being's spectral mystery,
The "why" of things about which humans cannot ask,
But only their flat "because" reply,
The plane dimensions,
Forming with a hoping, but yet forlorn imagination,
The "what" of things of fractal clouds,
The depth of the third dimension,
Which in us only lies,

In the self's prophetic soliloquy
On the lapidifying external nature
Denying, with a covert smile,
To solace the desire to know of mankind
Lured on by false hopes and semblances
That nature is like a mother
Giving all her fruits away
As a big, tall tree
Unfolding, too, the "how"
She bears them freely with plasticity,
The yearning, which often flies unwinged,
Of any inquiring being,
For mother Nature's smile may be bounteous indeed
In the awakening of our consciousness,
But, as a being-in-itself or an artist working from within,
She never unbosoms how the sun into the ocean dips,
As we ourselves, deep down within,
Are baffled in grasping
How sorrow to love gives in.

Of Human Nature

There is a method in chaos

As there is one in human madness,

Thus a paradise in every turbulence,

Yet no turbulence in paradise,

But in things it's an eternal recurrence,

Whereas in mankind it has no fixed permanence.

In the former it fades away

According to the uniformity of fractal nature

Just as roses grow again and again

In accord with its way

To send forth fragrance to human decay

Which can never the bloom of youth revive

Chasing butterflies on the lilies of the valley;

In the latter, instead, it aims to follow

The restless and diverse course of human bondage,

To let the living be born

To accept an uncontrollable fate,

A devised merriment of the gods' folly

As toys and puppets of the world's doleful stage

Fighting senseless games with fast and lethal weapons

Only to leave parents and perhaps the species

Bereft of any progeny,

Like one's symphonic lament

For the sons of no one in Barber's Adagio,

Or like the common chant does say:

L.B.J. how many kids in vain did you kill today?

Playing ruthless games on each other's feelings

Until we have quenched our sadism and masochism

Along with self-destructive hate and selfishness;

And torturing nature with scientific enterprises

To discover the chemical elements

Of life and reality

To which she gently responds with her sibylline smile

That no crucial element carried out

Can succeed in finding her out.

To modify this sublimated violence

There is little remedy,

For different and mutable individuals are doomed

To repeat such *civilized* bestialities

Without ever learning from self-corrective natural beauties

Their displayed patterns of love for harmony,

Although only chaos might be seen in the beginning.

Ah, if only mankind could manifest in its destiny

Those instinctive and virgin qualities!

They would defeat the unwarranted purpose

Of ungodly authorities as travesties of justice,

For their paradigm is the true light for genesis

Which drives humanity out of her fiendish misery

To respect one another with humane dignity

In breathing their vital breathing freely.

Crossing Swords by Misunderstandings

Without blurring the class struggle,

But clearly speaking without regretting,

Why do we still march on

In crossing swords by misunderstandings?

Worldly people have done so,

Let's not forget,

With A WILL TO POWER from the cradle

Making "heroes" from the scourge

Of their greatest bestiality

Ruining humans with wounds and evils

Which can never be healed

And our dear ones gone forever

That the heart cannot forget.

Within the macrocosmic strife of empires

Breeding in the crimes of DIVIDING AND CONQUERING,

And thereby calling "civilized,"

There is the mad battle of microcosmic ego-powers.

In defending their DOGMAS, the latter

Are not as swift as the former did

In taking up arms and the barbarians wiping out

For their camouflaged PAX ROMANA,

For their cross-grained claims

Have more personal aims
Of selfish and swinish games
Alluding yet to no universal sways.

The whims, the ideals and passions
Of humans' dramatic microcosm
Long for implementation and satisfaction,
And for this very violent passion,
No matter how a person
Is so close to another,
They will speak to each other
By always intruding their worlds
Upon one another.

This is the public spirit of the social animal,
The Dasein who paints the same verbal canvas
And shares, with compassion, common customs
With other cultural microcosmos.

There is a greater talk still at cross-purposes
In the belief of human illusion,
And thus followed by delusion,
Of sharing a deep understanding
In the primary ties of the DEMOCRATIC GROUND
On LOVE and RESPECT for others founded.

The lover and the beloved

Because of their smoldering "Eros"

The core of their feelings seemingly interlock,

Yet their words belie their truest RIVAL PASSIONS

By often for the shadow

Their substance sacrificing

Or below

The threshold of consciousness hiding,

Likewise two rival countries

When for a place under the sun scrambling,

Sublimating them with a double or politic talk

Lest in revealing their repressed crux

Will pay the price of being scorned.

The intellectualist elite, instead,

Wherein reason should reign supreme,

Engages more often in misleading talks

Than those whom it attacks

For the art of reasoning lacking,

For, from among the highbrows,

Who have molded their personal views

According to creeds and fixed views,

If anyone chooses to offer one view,

Thousands of decisions and revisions

Are made by the impugners

Until little agreement is exhumed,

But a long micrology at cross-purposes is pursued

Neither as a mad pursuit of ventures of ideas
FOR CHANGING THE WORLD,
NOR FOR INTERPRETING THE TRUTH.

This is the merit of glassy and radical "Rationality"
Engendering so many misunderstandings
In a plastic society where man makes man
As to let, at first, a CHAUVINISTIC VISIONARY
Cross swords against his bosom friends
And then, like a fast bird of prey,
Swoop upon the "civilized" world
So as to make a bloody, intellectual "history"
Even for the peacefully benighted race
In fettle of inward lethargy thought to graze.

The Celestial Sphere Amid Violence

When the fiery and brazing sphere

Warms me up to venture upon a heavy fate

Under the windy and cloudy sky of the "Big Apple,"

Sleepless as its unsteady wind

Which not only the trees sways but bends us in a stream

To paint on the wall of conscience the wanton deeds

Before dries up the fresh plaster of its true fresco,

The ravages of the nuclear bestiary of the times,

Of the century the greatest HUMAN BESTIALITY,

Too diverse and deadly to be concealed,

Too hideous to make the dead lie still,

As those lethal "scuds" and flying basking sharks

Ripping through the scuds of the oversea skies

To be sown in the fields of Mars so as to reap

From them bloody harvests of countless human toys

Rending the air with loud, piercing cries senselessly

And, dimmed with tears, the care-worn heart of mothers;

Tyrannizing yet over our tyrannous hate

Against its grim, ferocious face of eternal vigilance,

Weather-beaten of blood, unbeaten and adverse

To any lovingness or serene coexistence

And never convicted by its own conscience;

A ray radiant of hope above the horizon of the back-stage

Invades my thought, with horror shuddering

By accepting firmly the human spirit's polarities,

And inspires into its fearful wandering some fight

To attain in a hell's despair the Eden, the heavenly armour

With a zealous entreaty coveted by my thinking ghost,

Circulating and doubting in our self-moving machine,

By nagging at its brain in the hope of finding out

In its organic labyrinth of loneliness

The winding course of my self-sown destiny

To illumine it with a streak of stars more often

In its temporal but steady effort of survival;

Though bereft of a tissue of lies and enormous vices

Which is the worm of conscience condoned by the world

Even when it horrifies and is uglified by

More turbulent and tormenting facts than Bacon's art,

A deliberate deafness to suffering,

Just like Stalin, crimes, terrorism and "crack,"

The radical brutality and rottenness of human craft;

Toward a lot of ephemeral, heroic and sublime, transports,

Through the conscious illusion of Art,

Heartfelt and eternized like the Divine Breathing,

Never moving into the void of the infernal oblivion

Where the beast in man's weary and deranged pondering

Of monstrous visions of shambles,

As of Auschwitz or Nagasaki...!

Is rescued from the acute outcries of the living conscience,

But ever Itself-thinking in all infused.

A Flight at Sundown

As the big steel kite
Like a soaring eagle
In the unseen air goes into a climb
And crosses the cirri crowning the earth,
A light blue dome vault breaks high above
In contrast with the vertical visibility of
A deep and dark greenish-blue one below,
Whose far horizon
Looks like the celestial equator
Of a curved space of unknown dimensions
By a smiling sunset painted crimson.

The continuous ascending left me panting,
Against the semilunar sun setting,
Before the sudden and veiled awareness
Of a twilight eternity
Under the shadow of its dim immensity
Of an infinite stillness,
Like the last sleep,
With little bearing
On the mass point left beneath.

I began to feign a fixed edge
With phosphorescent orbs laden

To check the deep anxiety I was possessed by

Deepening as time nonchalant was flying,

Incapable of facing that hazy Nothingness ahead

Like an ostrich my head in the sand was burying,

But to no avail it was to screen from

The wrench of that external and eternal reality,

For the seeming firmament continued receding,

While my shivering body burning like ice

Goading me

Into letting myself go of my senses,

As a flower terminal and solitary

Broken off from the stem,

And roving about the main of the boundless

With a lofty fancy without boundary;

And so I made the leap

In the shoreless dark in a random ecstasy

And found how sweet it was my shipwrecking

In that vast space odyssey,

Since, discontent with the world,

It reunited me with the universe,

But suddenly its joy was shortened by the emergent landing

On the earth's face ever-changing.

Song at Dawn

When the dewy night had fled,

Over the Tower's supine scar,

You, shining morning star, from your evening glitter,

In a clear sky more beaming were rising solitary

With varied songs of variegated solitary sparrows,

Harbinger of a little angel

Seeing the light through tears

Unvanquished yet

By the bleak thought and sour taste

Of the arcane fate,

As arcane is the whole universe,

Seldom with twilight joy bedewed or shaded.

More flaming than the sun's which stirs all creation,

Your light of hope fuel for human love

Refractory be not, oh generous goddess of the heart!

To the callow dream which knows that feeling

With a smiling and winged destiny

Unaware still of a life of violent ills

And of a farewell to the spirit tranquil,

Yet swarming and quivering blushingly

When with passion seized

With nameless longings thirsting for glory

And with a great many delightful mistakes

Overshadowed by the kaleidoscope

Of risky palms of glee and transport

Which only in the course of time are colored

By a shade of twilight tears of calm love;

Otherwise it would soon creep in

Our frailty and unknown old age

And the shade of the still and icy grave.

Thereon with your fair beam of old,

That kindles up with the sun the lightless earth,

Don't deny to the feverish and yet fertile fancy

Of virile feats by its helpless offsprings,

And to their fragrant memories,

Your shimmery, firm guide of love sifting

Into their soaring souls of virtue with life teeming

Facing nature, in appearance benign,

But always hiding or unkind

To their woeful and beseeching lyric of Sappho

Magnetizing and anchoring them

To its supernal beauty with coruscating wit,

For it would gain victory the dark distrust,

Enervating the fabric of life slowly,

Over your animating glory,

And thus one rises to say along with Quasimodo:

Why wasn't I born a soulless gargoyle

So as not to be by noble feelings decoyed?

Or by that blend of noble feelings and misery

Destroyed?

Sunset at Key West

As I was lost in gazing

At the serene and far horizon

Run through by the sea-gulls' gentle flapping,

Where the westering deep-red ball was bold

Against few yellow-scarlet clouds across the sky

And with its evanescent flames brushing and painting

The sea crimson and with leaping yellow ripples,

Life and memories were radiating and recurring,

Since time immemorial,

From the core of that glorious helium.

One but not long vanished human image,

Whose romantic pen masterly depicted this sight

And of its sun-burned fishermen's

With a Nobel Prize,

Crossed my mind and hinted at

His burning lust for life:

If you wish to live with meaning or bravely,

Have the guts to carry through,

Either for you or humanity,

What you really feel you can do

So that when life fades away

As quietly as this waning sunset,

The spirit may go to rest

Quietly without shame with the oars' pulse measured.

This is what Hemingway knew,

But Papa did not it to the end pursue,

For it is not a plain sailing

To lead life till the end, nor to be "defeated" ever,

No matter what one can do best,

As sweetly, at Mallory's , the bloody sunset suggested.

Without caring in what quarter it was sitting,

The evening breeze was rising

Refreshing me from that sea-scented, elusive sight,

While the sun was smoothly sinking,

Like a drink below the belt at Sloppy Joe's,

Into the fiery and briny deep

Upon which on its even keel

The keels were rocking it to sleep

Reminding me of the ghostly skeletons

Of the tall ships rocking in the cradle of the deep

Which valiantly wrestled for the key

To the Coral Reef,

Regardless of the risk

To sink down into the ageless beauty of its abyss;

For neither a fiery sun

Nor a fiery brine

Nor a fire in the island

Could prevent its old salts' fiery spirit,

As the old man of the sea,

From persevering in keeping its indegeneous seafaring

In the most stormy times of adversity

Until the sun itself

Would burn them, as cigars, to ashes

With the unquenchable belief

That their spirit of marine life

With the sun also rises

On the southernmost place of the U.S.A.

Before Supino's Hills

Oh delightful brows relieved

Against the ridge of high, steep mountains

Of my once tranquil and naive nest!

Woody and refreshing, and still more

Bestrewn with poignant wailings

Of canorous sparrows flying and nestling

Amid the velutinous and serried leaves

Wherein the sun-beam fails of

Overshadowing itself, but only when

They are swayed and winnowed

By wanton and bracing winds

Trembling through the branchy trees!

So much glee I used to feel,

And I still feel in my fugitive visions,

In going up and down

And then even rolling down

On your florid and dear breast,

Without ever feeling any shame

As when one goes up and down

Of other people's stairs

Of life a humiliating, vile and wailful pain.

Frankly,

Even before the flickering vestiges

Of your earlier sylvan shadows,

You evoke an ambiguous and vague sorrow,

A sweet sorrow without pain,

Like the surrealistic, enigmatic spell in the scene

Of a musically chaste and silvery moon's light

On the ripples playing of a tree-fringed lake

In between the abyss of joy and sadness

Leaving one without a strain of bitterness

But in the quiet recollection

Of its fairness sublimely listless

Bathed in the night and day's timeless stillness.

Once my gaze was cast on the opposite direction

Wherefrom I stood with my lonely and bosom friends,

The elderly trees of these wind-swept hills,

Glowing with grayish–green stocks and livery

Of rutilant and Titian shades,

Whizzed oddly a wail

Amid the foliage's rustling

And suddenly their growing wail,

Like a tail breeze with grace,

My frame embraced

Trying to hold in check its thinking process

Which their present nature was comparing

With another under different skies far-away,

For they were craving for speaking

In this manner:

"Where are you going with those impish eyes?

Must you be leaving already to resume your hectic life?

Why are you not tarrying awhile in conjuring up

Visions of your snapping of some tender sprigs

And in tasting again

Our sweet, lusty and grazing breeze

Up above our heights

As was your wont to do with charm

With your daring briskness of boyish pleasantries,

Like that of the querulous tenants of our branches,

Vibrating the soul with fresh passions

Enduring in no way a harsh stay?

Yet it was never, as nowadays, a repugnant force

Deleterious to our natural course;

Indeed, we know too well of your head,

Uprooted from our arms' brooding screen

Which, in your green years, so much it protected,

That just now is coming back,

By feeding on dread,

From far-off lands

Loved by now as one's motherland;

Besides, amid many a theory in your field

Has been said that,

Were it not a theater of ghosts,

Our dear ones driven out of the fold

Laughing bravely and of no fixed abode,

From whom we have been perceived of old,

Neither sorrow, nor joy,

In searching their preconscious memory,

Would cherish for our faded memories;

Nor yet for our present russet and seedy dress

Crowning and wooing these azure hills

With other verdant and leafy crowns of saplings

Upon which, like whirling wheels,

Are fluttered a riot of colorful, vapory images

For those beholding them in the distance,

And with one voice sighing a restless, vital breathing

Searching through their clothing and souls

To unbosom to them the root of our harsh sorrow

For having been left forlorn, chagrined and pithless

By the wry pollution and inventiveness

Of subtle monsters

Of the twisted and fierce flights

Of the morbid, modern fancy

Searing and stifling one's conscience

And the tasteless and colorless lymphs blackening,

And not by a flourishing one alive

With a deeply implanted love and Liberty style

Quickening it with the inner sap to create

An environment with far-sighted remediations

Lit by the riant sun,

Unvanquished and life-giving still,

Which its cathartic and hot scourging beam

Silences, tempers and heals

Any decadent being in a sink of iniquity
Who is blithing our scented joy of living
With a wormy slogan of conquering nature
No less virulent than the one
Of change in human nature
And causing us from his wanton satanism
Quietly to languish,
A canker in the bud gnawing all of us, the living!!
Yes, all of us, the living, far and near
From these holy and secluded hills."

Thus, at that, they left me
With a sore heart,
Since their rusty murmur of poignant grief,
Fainting away in the distance within their deep valley
Nestled between the lofty mountains,
Is our life-long grief,
And that, can neither be depicted,
Nor shadowed forth by another's grief,
But only felt
As our slow and wailing combustion
Of our orphan, glassy and vile existence
In our present vale of tears of violence.

The Circle Of Life In America

Oh circles of the unity of life!

Spiral or concentric,

Expanding or receding friends,

We are all circumscribed, no doubt,

By the grace of the Alpha and the Omega

With no beginning and no end.

While our circles are temporally flowing

With an inner passion for life

In the midst of the timeless and shoreless Unknown,

We are also in quiet despair struggling against inner circles

Within the greatest sphere of human violence,

The bestialities of our century's egocentric circles

Selfishly deviating from the centripetal soul force,

Or centrifugally, at once, flying in two directions,

Like a sadomasochistic epicene

Not knowing the sense of belonging

Nor to which quality of living

Who has a deadly polar identity

Of foisting on other subject wills toward their centers

Its arbitrary authority or will

Inflicting far more barbarous sufferings

Than the ones falling, in the nadir of human progress,

To their tragic star aimlessly.

We The People have the right to ask:
Where is our epic, eccentric circle,
Wreathed with the halo of the sanctity of life,
Which takes the lead in that direction
And restores a salutary wind of political personalism
Over the wild and endless prairies
Of America with coyotes howling
Instead of sepulchral, howling voices?
The yearning dream; not only
Of the first and brave Americans
Whose belief in the spirit of the wind
Amid the Wild West's green ruins
Is haunting still with a ripple effect
For wounds that can't be healed,
But also of all races in the land
Of the last democratic hope;
Which sweeps away the clouds with depths of misery
Saturating people with a depressed rain
Of inhuman debts in the midst of plenty,
As the dead weight of hunger and poverty
Left unchecked, if not, by prevarication, created
By the vicious circles of rumbly and feckless leaders
Who tell people to read their lips of doublethinkers
With no service of concentric vision
In fostering the cause of us all
As circles of a rainbow on the new horizon
After the heavy tax of an undemocratic storm
Or taxation without representation.

A Tribute to a Dream

Those who are now enjoying
And have long enjoyed Justice,
Not only since the Greeks named it DIKE,
But from the State of Nature with no transgression,
Forget that, for a rift of it in the clouds,
Mankind suffered or the supreme sacrifice made
And cannot taste nor appreciate
The deep meaning and need of it
As those who won it from Serfdom;
So it goes for its twin sister, Freedom.

The burning question of the bush then is,
As it was down the cold-hearted ages,
Whether we are at heart, as in joy and grief,
Extremists for the sake of injustice like terrorists,
Or extremists for the cause of Justice
Which its spirit is still in a stage
Of pilgrimage and crucifixion,
For we cannot escape History, in spite of ourselves,
In the vigilance of its memory searching our conscience
But we are all subject to its timely process
And not to those who make it with direful dogmas
In a globe without light of its own
Filled with gases of inhumanities and iniquities

Which no longer must our conscience stifle and sear.

Not caught in the trap of the will to power,
Of the treacherous, human bondage, for the mighty soul
Is in an agonizing torture! but with a willpower
Tossed and tantalizing every night
In a fiery trial on a feverish bed in chains
To make or not to make the long awaited escape
From the shackles of a woeful ignorance of the past,
The fear of the fighting against inequality in freedom
Or of daring to know our present conscience,
The hardest thing to hold down to in democratic nations,
As the Spirit of the Wind of the Red Indians
Has wisely uttered from the virgin wilderness
Violated by the lawless Wild West,
For raising the rotten corpse of whited sepulchres
To the threshold of a wholesome dignity
By those humanity's soldiers with the content of their mold,
Like the soulforce of a true King of peace
Ready to face with passive resistance for his dream
Of fair coexistence in joy and in misery
An untimely death, the human common denominator,
As a prophet ingeminating to sue for justice
With a sleepless strife not only for a time but for life
As the sure way to feel free existentially
From the ground tyranny of grim dreamers' ideologies,
For a kingdom plagued with sordid violence within

Throttling the dream of letting freedom ring
Has nothing to offer to the undaunted voice of the living,
But only death as the only remedy
To the slow combustion of their suffering
And, at least, the sleep of the just sleeping.

Thank You, Gorbachev!

After the prelude to the Cold War,
Threatening to return the world to ashes
With the lethal monsters of the sleep of reason
As an apocalyptic vision of man's greatest bestiality,
Europe's whilom, blood-drunken battlefields
Are haunted by the ghost of a Russian phoenix
Rising with a keen and new dream
Of the standard of peace and deliverance
For unequal peoples who suffered equally
For the same reason
Under the yoke of the Wall of Shame of Berlin,
Of the butchery of ruthless despots
With their belief of absolute certainty,
Let alone the meaningless living
Behind the dire Iron Curtain
In their despair and agony.

Let us hail, as a knight-errant, this zeitgeist,
The true consciousness of modern times
With the courage to be in this arcane life
With soaring "summits" towards a star-spangled sky
Shining upon the epic souls of nations
Witnessing, with their supreme sacrifice,
An unreachable vista of yore

For which rivers ran red with deep bloodsheds,

Yet a reality achieved today

By "Glasnost" or the dignity of man,

The glory of the Renaissance and authentic mind,

Whose insight in the creative freedom of mankind

Struggled against the violent source

For all our woes in bondage on the edge of insanity

Of effete ideologies as imperatives of cruelty

To ensure the pursuit of solidarity and faith

Not only in these current and joyful events,

But also in the womb of time

Which, with a binding oath, our souls tries

To live in harmony with one another,

For a life which has not gained free will,

Neither love, nor respect, nor dignity,

Was it then worth living?

Long live Gorbachev!!!

The Shadow which Still Pursues Me...

In my lonely wandering

Through the windy woods of Supino,

As used to do my father for rest at nooning

In the noon of his life when living,

I happened upon his once-youthful shadow,

Wrapt in leaves amid a shroud of mysterious haze,

Bearing on his stark shoulders

His younger boy's loving burden with good grace.

In a fog of doubt filled with fright,

I queried like Hamlet

On the tower of the castle:

Are you a turbulent ghost,

My being's chaos?

Or an endearing phantom of my thought

Haunting me of old?

Or goblin at my fallible eye

Poking fun fleetingly?

Tell me,

You that chase still the fatal shadow of the living,

Are you touched by the hid and quiet breathing

Grazing and caressing me with mildness

As you once in your breast

Clasped me with deep tenderness?
Which twines and quickens the dead leaves
Changing their inertia
Into a rustling and swarming of living nature?

If your wraith is the cold shadow of a shade,
Why dare stop me from my free gait?
Ah, perhaps I got it!
The spirit of the wind is your veiled angel,
The form of your reflected shadow
Invisible as the sun's splendor,
Your vivid voice of once
In these sacred places of mine
Whispering me that the shelter of prayer
Is the sanctuary,
But the shelter of love for your departed one
Is your torn heart of any sunburst bereft
Reawakening shades of grief
To the troubled mind's eye
Every time it treads again
The tender traces of things past
Without even a ghost of chance
To stave off the cruel current
Of that human lot of bloody teardrops
UNTIL THE STREAM OF THOUGHT
Is stanched by the still of the grave.

To an Ideal Mother

In the dusky shadows of evening,
In the impending woeful odyssey of the living,
But above all in the shadow of suicide
Looms before me the living marrow of me
Of my dear maternal, wistful shadow,
With her glaucous, tearless, but foreboding eyes
In wavy black-haired enframed,
Under the shadow of my absurd, forlorn silence
To break through, with her obstinate, life-giving love
Beaming with faith unshaken,
The shades shrouded in gloom
Of the soul with agony wrung
Labouring under an unjust and unhappy desire
Which Christ once with His sorrow of love ransomed;
And to beg without ever holding herself aloof,
But always in her lowly and bleeding human testimony
With upcast eyes heavenward pleading,
Like a pelican's immolating and selfless piety
Piercing even a heart of marble through with its fervency,
That elsewhere my thought switch
Towards the placid and blithe memories when a child
On her tender lap dandling rhythmically
With her impassioned singing of dreamy melodies
Which fairly and swiftly the heart seized,

Charming all its fears away then

Of the cold shades wreathing it dimly

In the flush of its bright ardors dreaming,

And nestling it to slumber on her sure bosom,

While breathing into it hope for an unsure future

Known to her more than her own creature

Among labor pangs, war and mournful events stricken

Leaving her young widow and sad in appearance

Without ever repining like a humble and loyal servant

At the Divine Providence, .

But, in spite of that, with the daring still

Of a mountain flower of the Roman country

To steep slopes clinging with leaves whose veins are like streams

And at the rising sun reviving and scenting,

Always ready to change,

With an untiring heart full of proverbial wisdom

As when "the devil flatters you when for your soul hunts,"

Hate into love and every darksome, aggressive instinct

Into a sorrowful, yet loving existence fused by dreams

Smiling in the eyes of the motherly rapture,

Lidless and care-worn,

At the first triumphant, twilight glow of the morn.

Who Am I?

In the struggle of the spectral and normal life
To know oneself or the inner beauty of one's divine
In not a childish task of knowing one's name
Or of looking at oneself in the looking glass,
For one's eyes are not the soul's windows
As often has it Socrates' serpentine wisdom;
Yet one must try to find out the oracle of freedom,
Regardless of the risk of the later screams of dread,
In confessing, by life against the dread of death measuring
From his or her soul's dark recesses of blues delving
In which the mass of mankind in comfort is wallowing
As the maternal womb of unconsciousness,
How one not only with an identity crisis appears to oneself
But also how one stares with a fixed thought at oneself
When the threshold of consciousness crosses
And lives, by widening and deepening,
The Promethean conquest in its fluid complexity
As a bundle of feelings and impressions that makes
The concept of the ardent nature of oneself
Shaded against the background of the infrahuman silence.

If my father was the front fashioning shadow
And my mother is the rear resilient, flowered shadow
Of this real baffling page of life of a disease of feelings,
I am its living, plastic edge of their congruency,

Born between their love and secret sorrows

Mirrored in the nostalgia of the Roman church windows,

A disciple of strolling fire from the brave New World,

After I have, in the light of the faint hope,

My wild oats sown, often torn by the shadow and anxiety

Of life as the price worth paying for being alive,

Always on the edge of uncertainty running the race

With a poetizing, twilight thought in a responsive silence

From its primary plasticity, smoldered by the stinging echo

Of the existential care in search of a glimpse of harmony

With a disquiet violin laboring to dig up from darkness

Disquietful, artless beauties with a shining message,

Made up of a drama of recitatives and arias endlessly

Diffusing on the air their sweets tonic and single,

Through which it yearns to declaim against and foil--

Not by trashy toil, molding only an estranged conscience,

Of vapid, abstract and absolute talks

Of ideologies or forms of art

Wherewith one knows like whited sepulchres or robots or Faust

Only the cold system of love with no word of the heart

And does not love or act for love or humanness of life--

The saturnine miseries of mankind and for its sake

The pain of aloneness accepting to scourge and explode

The vices of injustice and the orgies of crime,

An irresponsible life not worth living of a base mind,

Rampant about the nakedness of our self-conscious times

Of indifference and of blind or fallen, bleeding lodestars.

93

A Portrait of a Young Artist

Without sickening praises
But in a subtle sense with unstudied eloquence,
By appealing to the sensible qualities,
She is, indeed, a human craft made of sensibilities,
Not to speak of her sensational sense of humor,
Gentle to people with a sane common sense,
Yet more congenial to those
Having a real bent for the arts and artistry,
Not cramping one's style for cranking out a stereotype,
But ready to receive her talent in the fashion industry
Confounding the skulls of indolent designers
Through novel and bold and fashionable statements
Molding, with an elegant and plastic grace,
A shapeliness of harmonious colors
Out of an amorphous piece of fabric,
And thus named, by right, an epoch-making maverick.

This is Cindy, a sweetie from Pennsylvania,
Living in New York, the sleepless city,
And, truly, it is the origin of her natural beauty
Which shapes her walk in urbanity
With a round head with a fleece of hair
Shining with black locks over her petite oval face
With dazzling, star-like eyes,

Green as the green-clad hills of her countryside,

Reflecting the verdant blossom of her kind heart

Often prone to allay another in sorrow,

With a mesmeric and enigmatic smile,

Forbearing it from any sad feeling of tomorrow

In beating out of it the daylights,

As in displaying brilliant techniques in her craft,

For the former, too, is a form of art

In bringing about a sight for the gods

To any unhappy creature who feasts his eyes

On her ingenious and increasing endeavor

Within or Without.

Change of one's Fortune

How hard is it to grasp change
But the more so to accept it,
For to change our scrap of life
One needs a fluke, or more, blind
To remedy all life's chances left behind,
The unconscious fate, unlike destiny, led without aim.

A daring angel's fortuitous and transitory heart,
On wings of love sweeping the serene
To rest upon the breast of the sleepless city
As the visiting swan upon the helpless breast of Leda,
Perhaps to reprieve another from fright came
That had the inbound urge, as that of waves,
To express and bestir its wildly kind, inmost feelings
With the unrest of its inmost, intellectual reasons
Insatiably the shores of the restless seeking
By denying changelessness as a state of death
On earth and in deep space.

A new life began at her first voluptuous embrace;
Oh what a passage, what immediate passage!
What indomitable and endogenous, strange sweetness
Came from her felicitous expressions
Of refreshing and fleshy frailties of purity!

What a revelation or serendipity there is
When true individuals their personae throw off
Like a vanishing mask of quiescent frost
On the sunny, golden and pure bosom of sands!
That I hoisted instantly the anchor
Holding me still amid heaving billows
Of blood burning and throbbing in my veins
To run my ship across her curvaceous breast
Heaved with unaffected, pristine shudders,
Deep and deeper swimming the shores of the deepest,
And then floating again to the surface
To taste the dewy morning's exhaustless freshness
With her winsome and quivering whisper,
"I will smother you with my sensual kisses
And consume you with the estrus of my passion
Exuding from my sultry body and erogenous touch
Until I have come off your shivering loins;"
And yet, because of her gusto for the forms of beauty,
We soon the anchorage left
To rove the hectic city laden with oddities
And tied ourselves to each of its modern sight
For being overwhelmed by riots of our joyful kisses
That we could hardly, from the site, the course speed
In the vaulting pulse of their feelings
Until the transparent haze of the twilight
Swifted our route to the hankered harbor of evening
Wherein again we unleashed from our restlessness

The free play of our sincerest, wanton urges

Laying bare some of the mechanical emotions

Cherished namelessly in the pent-up unconscious

In an endless cruise of clinches and kisses

That she and I frantic with joy

In releshing the graces of their flames

Never wool-gathering were in this odyssey,

But, under the bliss of night of love,

Although two, in an ecstacy of one flesh we were

Like two luminaries in a syzygy

Where she as I and I as she

Read and sang so wildly well

A passionately mortal but continuous melody

Until death, we hoped, would bid us farewell

And make us marble statues in God's acre.

On My Departure

At high noon, looking away heavenward, I mutter:
Depart! depart! depart I must!
With a heavy heart
From the country of the fair "Si"
Vibrating, amid carols of birds, laden with glee
Across its sunny sky's azure geniality;
I depart as a craft without a country
Which goes from shore to shore,
Like the singer of the psalms who bore
The ark around from town to town,
Weighing anchor from the Old World
To return to the hospitable haven of rest
Of the brave's New World.

Yes, I am by birth Gemini
And perhaps also by customs and mind,
But this splitting of life
Is the doing of brittle fate
Which no deux ex machina
Can divert me from its irrefragable mandate
To follow as a variable my divergent line
From its predestinate starting-point
With my dear ones in common.

On the ground I left them in suspense
For my ploughing toward the uncertain,
A dead space without dwellers and shelters,
In search not of the ghostly kingdom of heaven,
But of the murky skyline of the grimy skyscrapers
Below the western bearings,
While behind the plane trailed a lonely wake
Which wrote with white wistful words:

Farewell! Farewell brothers of my younger age...!
I am going back to the endless prairies
Of my generous Indian friends
Who, for the Love and Sorrow embodying us all,
Like us are communicating vessels,
Unequal in shape
Yet in nobility of feelings at the same level,
Living not in a cimmerian past as sun-fleers
But with light,
Reflecting in a three-dimensional sphere,
In harmony with wisdom, music and faith,
Wherein even the parallels of diverse geometries
Will meet at an infinite remoteness........
Therewith, had we never met or never parted
We would never have been so broken-hearted.

To my sworn friend of time past, Carlo, and Canadian friends.

Memento of Canada

Hail and Farewell, tender friends!

Memento of a dear yore,

Of a common and bounden soil

Upon which daily foot

Our body sets no more,

But elsewhere nostalgically, and yet gladly,

It is caused to stay

Seeking fortune in the New Land of the brave

Wherefrom breeds the concept of universal stock

For the survival of races in a multicultural pot

Sharing in the joy and wealth of light immortal.

Resolved and receded in thought,

Like Michelangelo's ideas

Receded into the sentient block,

To return to your ancestors' "Rock"

Amid the beauties of the Roman Country's hoary ruins

With golden wheat and generous grapes glowing,

Yet, for all your heart's trials,

You cannot your struggling passions free

Nor the proud ties cleave

From the refulgent shore of your Canadian harbor

Claiming your undivided measure of devotion

To its fair, virgin snow-slopes

Which the glaring sun roses and thaws

As your heart also thaws,

After a glass of redolent wine,

For the fragrant memories enshrined

Holding the brave spirit in thrall to love.

As nowhere is a rose without a thorn,

So we must make the best of these both worlds

By ceasing to wander from one love to another

Or to play like a swinging pendulum

To and fro between life and death

And becoming , as Garibaldi, a hero of both

With the courage to throw ourselves heart and soul

Into the struggle for their same cause,

Freedom, the course of a true love,

Leaving behind those darling dodos,

Which thwart the vitality of our past valiant roots

Pregnant with our present and future,

By leaving no stone unturned

To reach yesterday unreachable,

A falling star fetched with an undying flame

Only by the Promethean spirit of the age.

To my glorious friends, Nick and Fortunata
A Weekend in the Catskill-Mountains

As I come out of the urban, dark woods

Into the open of a riant and halcyon morning

Of August, from the plenty of summer streamed forth,

The veil is melted away of my repressed silence

By the glazed sight lingering before my close friends'

Cozy, sequestered and nestled wooden cottage

Projected against the rising mountain walls about

Which some of them, shaping a huge valley,

Seem to encounter in some place

Each other in the form of a wedge,

While some, in some other, mirrored in the lakes,

To overlap one another as hugging old shapes,

Narrowed-leaved variously of soft and frosty lamina

Coruscating greenish-bluish shades

Wheeling on unequal, stellate crests growing wild

Of different and hospitable forest-trees

Weirdly beckoning me to carpe diem;

And somehow I felt naturally twined with the birds

For the mellifluous twitters of their carefree carols,

The spirited music of nature springing

From its panorama of small things of beauty

Which are to bigger things the prelude,

And even with the leaping deers' meek look

Little suspicious of human bestialities.

This is nothing short of a spontaneous relation;
But how could this be that one finds
Milk of human kindness in the wilderness?
That one feels no longer there the exasperation
And the nightmare of the gross apathy of the city?
How could one find solitude in a village
And loneliness in the city?

Maybe it's true that when one is benighted
Under this village's white light of the bright moon
Refulgent on diamonds of dew
Over immense and gusty plains of green strewn
Its mountains about do not ring to multiply
Distances, nor spaces and nor crimes
Like the monstrous, crystal palace walls of the city,
But one is in the walls of the heart enfolded
With the real medley of the candidly human community,
No absence of feeling, no longer the despair
Of alienation against human communication.

How beautiful it is the smell of refreshing Innocence
In the midst of this racy reality the soul sating!
Yet by many fain forsaken
For the necessary halitosis it fetters
Of a society hectic, plastic and "civilized"
For which a cure, perhaps, is the resolution,
Since there is no spontaneous solution,
In the return to the pristine life but "Humanized."

104

Life At The Edge

No more in the primordial maelstrom of the Earth,

Where once murky darkness brooded over it,

But marvelling still

At the most awe-compelling epiphany,

The wonder before the eyes of anyone "alive"

Nothing less than an eloquent adoration,

One cannot choose but to ask for its adaptation:

What do I know about life and its mutation?

Or where does its evolutionary stream begin

Of the double helix of DNA

From which, through the split second

Of Mitosis and Meiosis,

A new life wholesome rises

In so far it stands

On the edge of the blade,

But, if it should fall off

On that momentous second,

Amorphous it develops?

Doubtless, one is awake only to its sands

Swiftly into unconsciousness lapsing,

Maybe also to its agony of joy

Mingled with misery and violence;

Or to the child seeing the light in sorrow,

As there is no sun without shadow,

Which is the sport of his or her own fortune

Running across the chaos of the cosmos,

The dark and unconscious onus of fate,

Opening the curtains to the instrumental drama

With the recurrent theme of living for living,

People's follies on the world's prosaic stage of hustle

Who become humane with a personal destiny,

Yet unaware of its vital mystery.

To know the veil of this process of creativity

One must intuitively be able to see

Further than the forest and the trees;

Perhaps one's greatness should try to tear aside

The veil of its sinister extreme,

The debt of Nature,

The experience of which no human has ever had,

Nor of speaking in a dead language with the dead

In order to learn how to die one's own death

So that one might learn how to live bravely,

But only of the dread of its agonizing uncertainty

More smouldering and smothering than any happiness;

Unless one experiences the vital dust theandrically,

A human with a nature divine

Resurgent from the voiceless shades,

A defeated death yet unknown to any mortal

Who would come back from the ashes

To tell us about its arcane nature;

Nor could we be consoled as open-minded, accepting

Altho his synechism of the physical and the spiritual,

With the Gray Friar's prayer, who is the patron saint

Of all living things, that it is in dying

That we are born in eternal life,

For this is the quietus of the body

And the belief in the soul's immortality,

And not, as well as the Cogito of Descartes,

An existential reply to the paradox of life,

In which the subject is and from which thought begins,

By touching, both at once, its extremities

And its eternity by those in the living present living.

From its sea life of primitive but breathtaking absurdities,

Wherefrom also spring the goddess of beauty

Ebbing into a sea of uncertainties

For its Eros' sensual vagaries,

A daylight there is not

For a sleepless river of life;

Yet even the logically faultless skeptic feels,

For he, too, is a living river or a plankton on Earth

Raising doubts where questions cannot be asked,

The infused protean breath

Into the expanding universe's organic matter,

Or perhaps even into the half life of atoms

In an eternally self-reproducing universe,

The over-soul manifesting itself especially

In the breezeless shells of mortals in a lived world

By inflaming their frozen, elemental energy with

An ensouled brave heart weeping only for humanity,

Listless to transcendent contrivances

For saving the appearances, for only life can unfold life,

To the Unknowable and Boundless with no desire,

But with its agonistic faith and functional unity

Defying entropy and becoming ever more organized

In struggling from the living death with anguish laden,

As the "frozen music" of the sentient and breathing statue

Of Michelangelo from the restive, cold marble,

And conquering, without insisting on safety and security,

Through its own deep will of sensitive openness

To new experiences unravished by defense mechanisms,

As a dancing tissue in the great Becoming

Its various soul-states of loneliness beyond sadness

By harmonizing them with the glorious wine and brio

Of a new Eroica's rustic and jaunty dance rhapsody

And thus in the open air breathing the answer,

With its primary belfry spirit, of the unanswered question,

The unfading motif, forever unfinished and diverse,

Of fresh but inevitable and continuous tones

Of its oracular nature in its own soulful motion

Of self-affirmation across the mass of life's purgatory

From the month of November's melancholy:

That Life is the dynamic Art of the living

And living is the motile beauty of the fabrics of life

And of its ever pregnant endeavor at the edge of twilight

Weaved with the quivering rhythm of the Dionysian delight

In their creativity diversified from surging emotions,

The outer splendor engendered by inner tension,

Recollected in emotion, in joy or in sorrow,

For emotion breathes emotion or successions of impulses

And courage breathes courage to be and to know

And so a restless heart breathes forth with insightful acts

Plastic, restless forms, as a mother molds a child,

To express life's tantalizing images of polarities

Across them with its agility to leap and trill as a mean,

Or of human contradictions as concrete universals

Of illusions and reality or of unity and diversity,

And that's all what one's broad heart needs

To thrill itself with life's own manifold reward

In its most recondite, enduring and elementary strings,

Forlorn of pent-up emotion and of pleasure objectified

From amusement in things, as in a fierce war of conflicts,

Or in the future of an illusion turning into a delusion,

To break the boundary of extremities through

To a greater freedom of loving to distraction the spark

Of an emergent gracefulness as an ultimate concern

Which affirms its existence as a needful kind creature

And charms and kindles it with èlans of delight

Craving for the feeling pleasure of the imagination

In more permanent possibilities or points of repose,

Or in running, with a torch immortal of a kindly Titan

To be past on to other generations of mortals,

The marathon of life with a passionate will to believe,

Until its very last stirring breathing, the loveliest still,

Daring to keep on acting against the anguish of nothing

Whereby its truth fails to wrest the truth of life,

Neither making it a tragedy by monstrous feelings,

Nor a comedy of concealed thinking as in Dante's,

But in Falstaff's, the true spirit of life,

For it is its trill which pervades the whole universe,

Nor fruitless when painted gray in gray by stale theories

Colorless of it as the host of forms yet-to-be-expressed,

But, by clothing it in fine phrases, deeds and symmetries,

Reconciling it with its own humanity and recurrent dualities

A sea of beauties wondrous and luminous

Wherewith smiling with love the heart wins

The race within for the pure possibilities.

To Pat and Ted and Friends.

The Spirit of Festivity

Oh friends! Oh friends!

With a swelling heart of joy,

Listen from your heart,

To more pleasant joy!

To when the fiery flights of Pegasus

In the air of this yule-tide of gathering

The sacred brake of art stir

And the wit of its melic fancy

Floats and steers

Across the clouds and mist of immensity

In search of the mysteries of the stars

Above Us!

Hanging from the infinite ceiling

Of the temple of God

And over those of the heart

Hanging restlessly and uncertainly

Within us!

Yet, it's in the latter's sublime profundity

Where lies the one of goodwill,

The deepest in sincerity,

Unceasing Love!!!

With wings of humanity and logos

Forever soaring with luster

For the prospect of noble heights,

Sighing for smiling away the solemn grief
And for spreading PEACE in its journey of forgiveness,
The gate of a paradox in a violent life that knows it not,
Like a cooing dove in flight with the olive
Stark in shining white
Against the golden-visaged sun's brightness;
That kept, and will forever keep, us,
Oh gentle and brave hearts!
Together, I hope, with happiness,
All these memorable years
In singing the friendship of life
During these lofty and jolly gaities,
Overflowing with vociferous memories
Of youthful follies,
With roars of songs and laughter
And with those merry trills faroff
Of bagpipes and silvery bells
Tormenting our free flow of spirits gently,
While the tango-music and genial wines
Dementing our minds,
By sharing in the wealth
Of Light Immortal
Of Christmas and New Year.

Christmas

Throughout the cold cosmos glory, glory, glory!!!

Bells peal, peal the boundless, inward joy

Of this high night for whom all nations rejoce

And together exalt my brothers songs of Hosanna

With your heart, hands and voice

In revering the son of David!

The Lord of lords, The King of kings is born!

The Savior!

Of all gifts the greatest bearer,

LOVE!!!

Oh flaming children, to whom,

And not to the wise, nor to the simple,

Is its humble secret revealed!

Bridge the heart's long-felt gap

With the candor of its catholic and ceaseless sap;

Praise and raise hymns with the bagpipes

And with the Christmas letter

Read to the head of the family

How its ingenerate Messiah, joy of man's desiring,

On a rampant earth Peace brings

Without thinking scorn of becoming

A child of the human family

Perpetually stricken with tragedies and anxieties.

Tell your friends, near and far-away,

How Jesus, the divine infant!

Born in Bethlehem in a stable,

Like a lamb in humble fettle came

To redeem even the Gentiles

From a sinful state

And replenish our poor hearts,

Not how the farmer does with his garner

Only in harvest and vintage-time,

But with a goodness immortal,

Whose faith leaves us in a dauntless frame

Of sweeping before us all what is sad;

Of healing even the wretch

From a petty existence in harvests of war embedded;

In its forbearing link with hope resurgent

As a genial starlight within mankind

Steering every believer's heart

In this apocalyptic night,

By dissipating any fear of the dark

With its mysterious bright,

Toward the holy path of the Word of God

Writing a new law upon the heart

Which makes us all delightedly one and equal

In charity from our imperishable soul

Before the universality of the triune Deity

Of this refulgent cosmic event of solemnity.

A Thanksgiving-Psalm

Out of my heart's deepest recesses
I do confess, oh Lord, God of Hosts!
My quiet den in time of sorest distresses!
That my dead father's shadow
Might have come
In one midlife summer night's dream
To tell me to surrender my Philosophy-dream,
The consolation of the midwife of the spirit,
Yet You, that knows my folly and sins,
Have granted me the will
From Your Nature Naturing springing
To pursue and tend to my spiritual nature
Written upon the heart of the human race
By Your amazing eternal Grace,
The most luminous, intensest and truest lamp
Glaring down on my paved but unfledged phase
Like a lambent tongue of a bear
Licking into shape her cub's raw nature.

Forsake me not through this learning trial
Hoping to bear with enduring work and faith
Triumphant witness to Your glorious Charity
And cease not working on my courage to change
The shades of those things I can

And with serenity to accept and to be oriented by
Those ultimate things of the heart I strive for,
For to aspire to things that are for the immortals
It would be my soul's hell or everlasting loss,
But, with wisdom, let me know their difference
As brother Francis humbly prayed You for
To serve with joy his sentence to live in harmony
With Your uncaused will and virgin nature.

Within the shadow of Your wings
Many battles I fight and win
Against treacherous and violent men,
And You even let me win the war against them,
Not belying my thoughts and hopes
To vindicate what is often tardy in ringing,
The divinely earthly justice
Which is by all humans often forgotten
Yet forgiven by Your infinite mercy,
For to err and repent is human
But with sanctity You ultimately visit
The beast, Satan, in unfearing human shape,
Who in the beginning was Your adversary in Heaven
Doomed to wile by lurking in the shade
Your mould of human nature.

Likewise the haunting presence of the Sword of Your Spirit,
Often thought absent in my frail conscience and so in hell,

My comfort and rock was in my battles for life-survival,

Never expecting to carry, of course, the day

Against the debt of nature, but busy in its practice always,

For there is no providential escape from it

As Christ did to a miracle in atoning the fall of man

And crowned seated on Your mercy seat at the right hand;

Yet You have kept me from saying the last Miserere

When I was thrice with one foot in the grave

And made my wrecked life whole again

So that its strife I would go on tasting

In loving its unfolding star in a bittersweet pain

As a series of warlike preludes to fate

By accepting the grim reality of its nightmare,

While wrestling with Your ineffable Name

For my relumed breath by Your hope fed,

And yet, without giving weight to my smoke,

For my voice in these matters is not gospel truth,

I dare say in sincerity, for I know You will repay,

That to magnify openly Your Holy Name

One must be ready to bear one's cross gladly

Or to lose one's breath as a red martyr,

He who has the most devout and sensitive heart

For which suffers the most from the crafty, collusive fears

Wallowing in the maiming spiral of human artistry,

Since, in all matters, man militates against man

And naturally hates man and the cross of the son of man

And unstable is like his very vile dust;

Thus this cry of tears of mine

In this howling wilderness for You to consider

That are deepest in the human heart

Which is in deep waters with deep-seated fears

That its grieving face smear;

But, if Your inner light smiles upon the upright flesh,

Your creation not only without a subsistent pattern

But the opera of Your infinitely inwrought artistry,

Not yet his sun will set,

And his unremitting and splendid efforts

To fight or suffer for its white luster

With its divine glare on his erratic destiny

Will never a candle to the sun hold or be foiled,

No longer his cankerous source of dread quell,

But outshine even the Dance Macabre of the skeleton

And he will rejoice on earth in laurels

Making him in all his alcyon days sing

In that flush of reverent delight till his extremity:

"Deo gratias, oh Lord indwelling of the living!

It is finished! with the breathing of Your Holy Spirit!

Indeed, this was the heavenly manna of Your love

Healing every sorrow that earth cannot

And not from the shadowy hope of man or happy chance

I patiently waited for Your redressing chances

Which let me be a real bright rose

In the midst of sharp thorns

By irradiating the somberness of my frail nature."

118